# A Deeper Gift of Remembrance

# A Deeper Gift of Remembrance

Perry Douglas Sisk

PRIMIX
PUBLISHING
THE WRITE CHOICE

Primix Publishing
East Brunswick Office Evolution
1 Tower Center Boulevard, Ste 1510
East Brunswick, NJ 08816
www.primixpublishing.com
Phone: 1-800-538-5788

Published by Primix Publishing: 01/16/2025

ISBN: 979-8-89194-360-5(sc)
ISBN: 979-8-89194-432-9(hc)
ISBN: 979-8-89194-361-2(e)

Library of Congress Control Number: 2024922051

# Contents

# Flawed is cure

Perry d Sisk-November 023

Most Will Wait an eternity of their lives
In hopes of prosperity
Though fail to embrace or ever walk near
One measure of open charity
Those that see their conclusions for gone
Will all too soon forget
What was sang in one song
One wonders where did lyrics arise
That stir deep emotion
And bring tears to our eyes
Not so much when music applied
That enticed those who listen
For warned who was tried
When given their dose of humility measured
Forced to look past
What seldom is treasured
Some seem to know in advance what direction
To follow
Yet others will lack or hold to their lies
That they are so eager to swallow

Yeah adversity strengthens one's character traits
And also will look past
Ignoring those their Fates
Those who follow through
On their word one time stated
Look back to atone
For the pride so inflated
A reckoning coming will be well assured
The Affliction sustained
Will always be cured
Those flaws that we hide
Some take well in stride
That love for all others
Remain deep inside......

# One's self away

Perry d Sisk-November 2023

Oh there are times I share
My thought with me myself if I am sure
Yes indeed to better weed
Out those feelings so obscure
And my youth I id perceive
Those issues I did wear upon my sleeve
Knowing not what cause
A lot in company they would leave
So early on I'd hear a song
That gave remorse to thought
Feeling small though always call
To attention some had bought
I sought to learn to sometimes turn
And face this mirrored self
Hold grief inside and always hide
This heart upon a shelf
I also suppose I'm not alone
When keeping one repose
Though later seek one chance to speak
Of chapters left to close

Our lives are often seen as stories
Need be written down for cause
To go back and look what I had took
Yet never gave it pause
Seeking out just who to please
Always never left at ease
Those inner thoughts all come for naught
Once echoed in a breeze.........

# Meant to be

Perry d Sisk-November 2023

Do we not at times ask ourselves
Where has those better days to gone
Some search through books
And earlier teachings
To find one solutions
Perhaps written in a song
I have heard it said
That things always occur
In cycles and therefore seen again
If this were true
Why does a clear blue sky remained blue
And in the fall a tree seems to call
Does nature always mend
My inner vision unabated with years
That has passed some unrelated though why
I used to see folks getting along
With help of their neighbor's by and by
This culture now I see has lost
That one best known ability
To not just toss aside their pride

But rather look for love inside
More to see
That one instinct all knew to share
Not thinking twice
Out thought of care
Those days when people's moods were light
And look upon things with more Delight
May soon indeed come back around
When all will hear God's trumpet sound
Once again United as one
As was intended set forth
By our father and his son
All through the Ages
All waited to see
Just what it was
Was meant to be..........

# Truth to be told a nature Bold

## Perry Sisk-18 November 2023

In these early morning hours
I find myself again
These many thoughts race in my mind
To be announced with pen
Amidst these hours silent air
With stillness there
I find no will to cease
As thought I follow through on course
One pre-determined peace
I'm sure one day that some may say
For lack of things to do
All chores that most ignore
Of which I'd be guilty too
Attest I must to share a view
Some find is done for naught
For there will come a time
I see take pride in values taught
Being prone to lack some skills
That some will hold at best
Each day I pray to have more to say

And give these virtues rest
Our stay in life be at far too short
I often feel was cheated
Out of time enough to climb
Above what I defeated
In part and yet would I regret
Not having been allowed
That chance to cause
Or merely reset
That testament I once had vowed
A task half done and not completed
Would lend to wonder why
To even pursue for efforts sake
Does always reveal to LIE
Before I am old
One truth be told
Our Nature's were so bold..........

# Simple to see

Perry D Sisk-
25 November 2023

Things we enjoy
In our years that are waning
Simple as growing our gardens in Spring
Are there portraits we are farming
Some days in the early morning sun
There are walks to be taken
While always so grateful
Just to awaken
Some will find a humor
In these things we attest
These things our age do offer
Will soon all come to rest
As we watch the leaves of fall
Being tossed amidst the breeze
Crimson red the gold and bronze
Within the shade of trees
With waters of a lake so calm
And hours of early morning

Still as a sheet of glass
Reflects a sun so warming
All of those little things to often fail to mention
As does coincide our feelings
Among a failed retention
True though is told
To outlive one's usefulness
Far will outweigh
That better sense we bless
To lack a better desire to simply only be
So seldom taken advantage
The torment we hope to flee
All so simple to see

# A light to reach

Perry d Sisk-
24 November 2023

*There are some that say to escape*
*The confines of a season*
*Can be done with better reason*
*There have been those that stated no better*
*Fall from Grace goes without treason*
*Can time stand still*
*And yet still be measured*
*Within a dream*
*To know what is real by touch or by sight*
*Even by night does it seem*
*The gift of wisdom is nothing lesser earned*
*If not for growing old*
*Along with those years we burned*
*Some say our talents are taught*
*While some denounced the gift*
*Never having been bought*
*That ability to find our sole purpose for being*
*Should always be held onto*

*As thought never so seeing*
*There are those that lay claim*
*To always being used*
*They'll never acknowledge*
*Their own they abuse*
*Nothing ever hits home*
*When being forced to walk through the flame*
*When faced with a choice*
*To find ourselves to blame*
*Our lives short as they are*
*Hold an eternity of teaching*
*By far*
*So distant to take hold*
*As a glimmering shining star....*

# It is done

Perry Sisk-17 November 2023

How simple can it be
To find miracles to see
Each and every day
They are given to you and me
When I look up to the sky
And see those clouds
That are silent passing by
Some contain the rain
That gives the arid plain a sigh
To gaze across a sea or oceans
Vast and wide
Never take for granted that one
Who walks along our side
Since that day of Moses
As he handed down God's law
A man of humble stature
For a burning bush he saw
Why in this present day do people
So strive to escape their fate
Knowing full in absence of love

There always will be hate
For what has been just and true
Laid down upon our hearts
Give timely reminders of what's been gained
Or tossed and lost in part
Must never we forget to honor
What was done when our Lord put forth his son
Those back then stood Witness
To hear has been written
It is done......

# A promise abides

Perry Sisk-November 2023

Oh how those singers sang their songs
All about their rights
And oh so many wrongs
While many voice concerns over words
They simply will not hear
Failing always just to learn
How not to lose a love once near
Poets tell of gifts within
Though never given notice for
Often blamed by next kin
For fabric of heart they tore
Authors write their novels given
Present day or past
Never gave a relevance for
Their dream that ended fast
In older days are builders used
What nature could provide
With homes made out of logs and stone
A floor of clay inside
In light this progress so proclaimed that for the simple needs did pass

A longing now for what once was
Those flocks of sheep and grass
With man's Free will and always still
There's been one choice we lost
To know that we need not attain
Those things that bare no cost
Do unto others as one
Should stay that Golden Rule
This lamb of God so named was Jesus
That rode upon a mule
When people speak of end of days
They fail to always confess
No single man no angel above
Shall know that hour less
For not but one and too his son
Will one day there appear
As has been written
No more pain not one will shed a tear.........

# One's measure so taken

Perry d Sisk-
16 November 2023

In Retrospect yes we may all have been down
Darker roads that others
Giving the chance to change what was
With hope of better honoring
Our fathers and our mothers
Who it is still remaining of the living that's known
The gains and losses of giving
All who hold the capacity for knowing
What knowledge does provide
Far outweighs what wishes
And dreams one spirit may hide
For the love of someone we dare to not let go of
Have we not been moved by the grace of a dove
For those who view life
As one task yet achieved
Here with values self-taught
Some finding their passions compassions relived

No one is meant to know in advance
Their future when told
Further defined long after we're old
Those whom have withstood
Their own test of time
Relinquish or in part one measure of wisdom
Ones past will define
These lives that we lead
When looked upon in whole
Here that lack of reflection
Our existence had stole.....[for Valerie]

# Changes nothing

Perry Sisk-14 November 2023

With my vision growing dim
And a frame now standing slim
A sense of hearing
Far below acute
Unable to discern or distinguish
Any more the sound of a bird or a flute
That hair of brown once thick and somewhat curled
Now white and gray and thinner too
I still find beauty within this world
This loss of taste that prompts to waste
Once placed upon my tongue
Though yet to see what was to be
As songs forgot were sung
All tings do fade
Like noonday shade
That's cast upon the ground
And still along a lighter side
These dentures that I wear I hide
That smile I lost I found
I used to stand much higher than

I do this present day
And this final season gives to reason
One lasting view portray
To outlive purpose useful for
We see one plan in place
One up turned brow seen then and now
These lines upon my face
Have no fear what is near
One ending to begin
All these changes bring to bare
A love retained within.......

# One soul to ment thought wise

Perry Sisk - 6/11/2023

Something constant throughout Humanity I have come to find
There has always been the need to upstage
Each member of our kind
In hopes to attain that which is memorable
And always Everlasting
Those ropes that keep us tied unable to reveal
Those thoughts forever fasting
We feel it is better to be remembered
Fondly rather than forever loved or simply admired
Far best or have it said less calmly or made to conceal
Those feelings our hearts had hired
When all emotions come into play
Are there no more choice or voice to say
One's heart turned to stone
From a lasting decay or remorse
May one day still for recall of one's will
Reverse its darker course
Not solely for direction of a
Foreshadowed end
Though rather of a Harmony

Of another will to bend
One signal it seems to go unheard
And not so easily seen
As a fly captured cannot Escape
A Windows hidden screen
Gaze up into a cloudless night
Though stars that cast their brilliance bright
Are they deemed to be those many souls
Gone countless to the light
With time thus passed
In number to last
For more the Sandy Shore
Of every sea and ocean there be
The pain and sorrow he bore
In faith we have no need to touch
Or see for his love to be
Was meant for those Made in his image
One truth that all will see
Never a soul was left unmended
And some await his care
These older eyes that once disguise
This newfound wisdom there..........

# One seed of nature

Perry Sisk-12/11/2023

I find myself yet again
In silent contemplation of
Those years that fell away
As the petals of a rose losing fragrance
And color slowly fades
Though yet its stem will stay
This rose that was will linger there
Upon a stem still green
Given time with rain and shine
Of sun a new Rose soon is seen
Thus comes this revelation felt
Am I alone in this
One simple plan that nature holds
For dreams we one day miss
And in fact not oh too many seasons back
There was one pattern most would lack
A great uncoupling did I see
Began to fall in place
It seems so many all to eager
To want to join a race

I find it all too often though
To know from where to start
Whether matters brought to mine
Are always from the heart
This push and pull
This tug of war
Embodied frame of mind
Still in the morning mist we find
Forsaken for those blind
One need not have an eye to see
Nor sense to find what's sweet
What God instructs what nature holds
The colored Blossomed Street
Give him praise for lasting days
And youth we took for granted
On in time will past our prime
This seed that nature planted..........

# All that a mirror holds

## Perry Sisk - January 2024

Beyond this space and time erased
I now see captured upon your face
With tracks and lines that show those Vines
Of youth no longer can I trace
With eyes that now are Hallow
Of Visions they do swallow
Still hold to all that's been well earned one thinner brow
Somewhat silver now
Shown seldom raised concern
For those uncounted years
Which yielded all the fears
Of lesson yet to learn
So quickly gone left all dismissed
Not for cause but for those that still resist
That truth inside to know
What always comes about
A day that will arise to take
More than one to shout
Never has there been such a grander time than this
I come to find you did not mind

You were the one I miss
For in this face that I see now
Only serves to remind that forgotten vow
Once was spoken long ago
All that is written upon one face to know..........

# A second time to see

### Perry Sisk - January 2024

What things we see
So subject to change
As once the buffalo
Did darken the range
Flocks of foul
That would always head South
In the skies they would fly
So rare to see now
It seems that where man
Extends his awkward touch
Those laws of nature and Earth are revealed
To say no it affects so much
Some will say these Cycles come and go
And yet will never address
As to why some Winters hold no snow
How often have heard
There is something going on
All those things were used to know
Like stars before the dawn
Not so many we once could see

Across the night so clear
Hard to say what pluck them away
A sign that day is near
Given these things I see
And a past that I did witness
All of what there used to be
Will be what's more to miss
It really wasn't so long ago
As kids we heard it said
To ask our Lord our soul to take
Should we fail to rise from bed
So in my all to shorter span of life I've seen
Those landscapes Brown and Barron
That in my youth were green
In winding down who wears a frown
For what his kids have done
As soon to be
This world will see
Again his coming son..........

# For all he will gather

Perry Sisk-January 2024

Those who will affirm
Their denial for what is real
Lends to precognition
Of where and what we feel
Giving claim to holding sight
Of what is yet revealed
Does tend to show inner glow
For secrets kept well sealed
Prophets of old that boldly sold
Their dreams of what will come
Came at Great cost
For all they had lost
To many or to some
Or was it by chance
That some took that stance
To never be persuaded
Not to look to the skies
With their tear swollen eyes
And see the hate evaded
Forever is his love that he placed so high above

*Our spirits have to fly to reach*
*This is why we have his book*
*If we'd only take one look*
*And feel the word to teach*
*So many who did Miss*
*That heaven scented kiss*
*Of the breadth of his salvation*
*With valleys low*
*And mountains tall*
*He will gather Every Nation.........*

# A soul Direction

## Perry Sisk-January 2024

Here is something more
That truly needs discussed
Before the wheels we ride
Upon turns to rust

This things folks always called
Soul searching I don't think ever truly works
For canal is human Mind by Nature
So therefore fear of knowing always lurks

Honesty alone does never hide an evil past
To say we have all out lived what we have done
Is as a stone in which we cast

Even though we search our souls
That brings to True Confession
Who is to say those deeds not mentioned
Good or bad in their succession

With so many actions taken
There is but one true definition
All those facets of one Life
The many battles we did fight
To hide one inclination

A life so scripted so it seems
To later be recounted dreams
A number for we will never know
That sold that searched
One path to go..........

# Who walks our path we know

Perry sisk - March 2024

When made to look close
At an ever measured dose of reality held today
What comes to mind
What lies behind
One intended course they say

One taken on it all to prevent a fall
On swords that lack an edge
Always there will be
Kept for you and me
His son that made one pledge

This Earth that we inhabit
Is shortly lived at it's best
For all too small these numbered years
Had swiftly to our rest

Some may finds it sad and somber
We take our time for naught
While in his word so much not heard
That knowledge shared he taught

Each and every generation
Does steer so close yet miss Direction
For all that fell astray
Adjustments made be glad
He stayed
Beside us all the way----------

# The fire of conviction

## Perry Sisk-April 2024

Here now this I must confess
If only by conjecture more or less
I had hoped to do no harm
To those raised in cities
Or even reared Upon A Farm

For who is ever questioned
If morals are placed within a sift
What would fall on solid Ground
Or blown to an open sea adrift

For anything that sparks debate
Whether early or come of late
What frame of minds to celebrate
When questioned as to fate

Be clear of mind when found inside
That purpose for conviction
One hopes or at least to tell
One's duty dereliction

So easy to say
With utmost dismay
We seldom will make the call
Those ladders we climb
Or walls that we scale
Where pride is meant to fall

For those who asserted
What values deserted
That fabric a character holds
What is found in so many we ask
If there is any
Embers left among the coles----------

# On that stands alone

## Perry Sisk—January 2014

Who has not asked themselves
When will it be my turn
Then a voice inside so tells
There still is much to learn
Given that again to ask
What good is wisdom gained
This too said in later years
Disminished fears left strained

Seen through the eyes of those older lies
What souls alone will Harbor
What cares were cast into the wind
So distant and much farther
To pick and choose
Which one's to lose

Those cares for all concerned
Those feelings we bruise
That were mine or were who's
Their hurt we heal we learned

From people we know and family too
Never discount their pain
Never did see that love was free
When standing in the rain
That reign of love shown of the dove
That descended upon his son
Then that alone be set in stone
As to why he stood alone..........

# This thing a father keeps

## Perry Sisk-January 2024

There has always been
Times starting out
To try to just fit in
That ignorance of youth
That held less fear for sin
Always being told
By those older and wise
Always hold to truth
And give no credence to lies
Has anyone ever found in strange
That kids two or three
Knew to fear the kindness where
The older fail to see
This innocence of children seen
So precious in the eyes of God
Was it always more a ruse
Spoil the children and spare the rod
What was that one thing children knew
Before hey learned so late
Their nature to forgive was taken

In time bestow a fate
Time it takes in growing older
Is this what brings to harm
Those counted times I heard oh Daddy
Leave the light on
Did hold that sense of charm
It should come as no surprise
That why fathers love their kids
Any wrong done to his gift
Of children he forbids
In all too short a time it takes
For loss of youth we know
When born again a child of God
He will never let us go
So think it through
Next time we lose
A tolerance that we once had
That bundle of joy
That girl or that boy
That makes a father glad
The most treasured precious gift bestowed
A man and mothers all the same
For in that love wrapped within
Does never put out the flame.....................

# One end to reason

## Perry Sisk-January 2024

*In all of us there lies this fear*
*Of really never knowing*
*What knocks Upon our door and asks*
*Is there more this life stood showing*
*There will always be those casting doubt*
*Upon the ones with courage to shout*
*Stand your ground and don't give in*
*Never quit the race*
*You were put in to win*
*However and yet still though*
*It goes against your will*
*These years that follow suit*
*Makes us take that bitter pill*
*A guess we reach the age*
*Where we fear that Turning Page*
*That leads to that final chapter*
*Be the last we see as Sage*
*This book that speaks of many fails*
*Mixed with success turned into tales*
*Seldom do we find the gumption to ever*

Pass by one's assumption
That simply getting older we have earned
A right to be so bolder
We voice whatever comes to mind
Regardless ill intent or just be kind
Keeping mind the old have things to say
Just as kids are loud at play
Bearing our souls for all to see
When life leaves little more to be
One fuller span of life
Holds no chapter or no verse
To a song once heard so long ago
That viewer words would cite the curse
To live a life with one clear ending Beyond
That unseen course
With time not bending
For all we'll see what lives well past
A future not aware one future will Outlast
Always was this purpose
Intended should we ever dare
This I questioned in an ending
The countless ones that care..........

# The older wrongs done

## Perry d Sisk - May 2024

Folks expect the old
To be all so wise and knowing
So some of this may be so
So never allow them see
Your years your miles tread showing

Truth be told for old
Being wise is this
Truth departed from the lies
Is all there is we miss

Some put store and old wives tales
I have heard so many times
Knowing too when signs turn true
That seldom cross some lines

Good intentions being what they are
Sometimes can be akin to a door left ajar
One's heart knows not what temps it
Or tries to enter in
The rest assured as grandmother's knit
They know just where you've been

So fear of growing old
Gives to accept what must be
Just as eyes of the young
Saw farther what I now see

Try putting back where things belong
As changing lyrics to a song
To better match the base and tone
That betters the rights that one done wrong.........

# A prideful silence

## Perry Sisk-May 2024

Given that we have those
Who will always write the lines
Turning thoughts into words
Written down does more than paint the signs

The signs and wonders and simple living
At times are limits tested
Even the father did spend six days
Bringing all we know of and to being
And on that seventh day her rested

This common frame of reference
Here I give one solid preference
Near the Forefront of my mind
Those countless Souls asleep still seeing
The reason for their past lives being
In time it cannot bind

When called to rise again eternally apart from sin
Who of this life or of what comes after
Long after could want for anything more
That to hold that joy ang laughter

To find that peace within
We lost somewhere someway
That foolish pride was kept inside
Left nothing more to say..........

# Why the heart

## Perry Sisk-January 2024

In this Autumn season
Of this life that I have lived
I wonder if there will be
A greater gift to give
For those that aspire to accomplish better things
Do they ever in the distance hear
A bell that seldom rings
Then laden with mistakes
We have made through life so short
We wish we had taken time
To better this last report
For it indeed one's true accounting
For things we have done in jest
Or be admonished for the failure
Of knowing what was best
If all are seen for their feelings of the heart
So freely shared with all
Who dare to want to pick apart
Also aside from understanding
As Mortals always hold

*do often tell the difference in*
*A heart of warmth and passion*
*And those so bitter cold*
*Always said to judge with your heart*
*And leave the mind to rest*
*That sound of life was measured when*
*Was heard within our chest*
*Hard to explain how man and Beast*
*Were fashioned near the same*
*One has nature left to test*
*Though man will never tame*
*So in that grander scheme of things*
*That's kept for one to know*
*When looked upon for all we did*
*And said a record show*
*Always was it clear that within our final year*
*That second hand will cease*
*We will carry forth that love God placed*
*Forever lasting peace..........*

# A purpose far to hear

## Perry Sisk-January 2024

Music draws the spirit
In ways to draw one near it
Music calms The Rage within
That puts in place a state to win Voice
Inflection so randomly altered
That always will amaze
Though always inspect and try and dissect
Without any given praise
With sound so cast on the air
In waves received so pure
Omitted flaw and Essence saw
Perfection be the Cure
For music sooths and sets so still
Uneasiness known inside
With Angelic tones that brings us home
For want to always abide
For everyone wants a touch of what was
To feel that time of peace
That gift of Music given to all
That are living with love of our fathers increase

Music is that one Foundation
To bring to every Nation now
For not just in knowing the where
The what the when or how……….

# To see all that he sees

Perry Sisk-February 2024

Some will come to ask
Was he exhausted from his task
To share with oh so many others
Though born apart from Distant Brothers
Where we not all meant to be so seldom seen by those
Brought to the light of a recent recalled dream
Regardless of race irrespective of Creed
What goes without saying we all do hold a need
Throughout all of my years this one thing I have seen to test
Only when left with one recourse
Are we found to do our best
Why wait for damage to be done
To act and prevent what torments the Son
For indeed I feel that the father he cries
When he sees his children's soul demise
Awkward never be sure
If you truly were to be that one who did speak
To things we always knew as pure
A tear rolled down his cheek

*While standing in the mirror*
*Of those eyes he dried out tears*
*One God above sees though and image too*
*Regardless of the years....*

# A Hope of better judgement

Perry Sisk - December 2024

These are no longer the days
Of Andy and Aunt Bee
As that old saying goes
Few will ever see
A forest for a tree
If we pass to others
All we have been given
Any amount of anything left
For ourselves leads to never being driven
In these latter years
I need so firmly to print out
This self-prescribed determination
Leaves me to conclude without a doubt
Giving straightforward observance for all
That will hold these character traits
These pros and cons as it were
That sometimes we evaluate
Better yet and still I'll bet
It'd be a cause that seals Our Fate
Has it not been said that fear of condemnation

Should always lead to confirm
Our one and just salvation
In that one clear measure of
A total separation
Totally detached from Hope and inspiration
Solely defines
That stated declaration
On that day of judgement when
We hear I never knew you
Before it falls too late and we see
It all the more do his words
We did ignore ring so true
Thus for this very reason
We turn ourselves around
To his better judgement found..........

# In times and yet

Perry Sisk-December 2023

We are at the time now
Where we hear those rumors of wars
Were the people look up to the sky
Where the Mighty Eagle soars
Those of faith who still hold out
For hope of interventions
From the master of all who hear
Our call and prayer for better conditions
Tale us back to that time before
Such hatred and evil exposed
Itself out where in open air
So many sat reposed
Choosing not to see or deny
What was to be does not make it go away
If ever there were a reason to long for better season
Where signs he hears us pray
Being humble immersed in humility to know
There is that one to save us from fragility
Who holds solution to all confusion
Bring peace for all to see

We're it but for the one that gave
His only son
Our Hope and Faith not held in vain
From that he said it is done
Strength is not what is gained or got
Through those who would entice
It's finding courage defeat the urge
To walk upon thin ice
One strongest heart that shares in part
A weakness on display
So this day some will walk away
Though yet take time to pray
Still.. And yet……….

# A forward mend

Pery Sisk-December 2023

In cases such as this
Are there things that I did miss
When I look back upon my time
And await the thoughts that rhyme
I find that raising I was given
Gives me Faith for times we are living
To hold respect for who it was
Looking out for simple cause
We were taught to keep our mouths shut
And to always learn the laws
Laws of nature that apply to every season
Never asking how
Just know that there was good reason
We truly were a heaven blessed bunch
When everyday grandma made sure we had a lunch
Now granted for the time there wasn't much to pass around
But make do we did
And there our love was found
So simple that time it really was we would share
With one another for sake of just because

Bring glad for what we had
Though times were lean and often and
Keep in mind so often to find
That joy we found amidst the bad
Now today I am left to say
Not intended to charm or sway
I still see a remnant of
How our hearts felt back then
Though missed and alone for to have again
These memories of so long ago and then
We'll keep our future
On the mend..........

# One token coin

## Perry Sisk-December 2023

Well I wake up every morning and put some coffee on, I comb what little hair I have so thin and gray most gone, I fumble around and find my pants and socks that I wore, beside the door I find my shoes while wandering did I snore, my mind still fogy a dream I try to fit lost memory to, I can't help but think I'm on the brink of never seeing who, I used to be in latter days more able to get started, though nowadays to part those ways for me now go Uncharted, it is no surprise to await demise when usefulness is gone, but then still too with days now few there is still one job be done, find someone give freely to that holds far less than me placed high upon a shelf, I put there myself a token none can see, some would say a coin of sorts when gave to others by all reports, Acts as a key for both you and me to keep in mind we are all inclined to pray on bended knee, to be delivered from toil and strife this world does bring to bare, to make aware who is standing there beside us all our life this token bore a picture for one's face who all should know, the face of our Lord we all walk toward kept an eternal glow, for a season hold on and reason or ever questioned why he bore his cross his life that he lost for solely you and I..........

# Driven to task

## Perry Sisk-December 2023

Some I guess are prone to ask, what changes would I make if given
such a task, where would one begin is always a first concern, do
you go back to relearn those lessons we thought we had burned, up
in smoke and early on, thinking that we knew with every passing
dawn, just what plans to make mulling over and bite off more to
chew, if we could change that course of life we took, that know-how
that by which laid out and every book, found there in between the
lines that all two seldom did we take a second look, the things we
strive for that others may admire, with one lack of admiration did we
not pursue much higher, farther up that ladder we were told we are
made to climb, all the while ascending with our eyesight focused still
not knowing we were blind, to those ones set out to hurt or ridicule
and go as far to shame, those efforts we put forth we find who is to
blame, he being hurt and miscued then when young and starting
out, over time with no remorse grow bitter with thoughts of hate we
would shout, yelling upwards to the sky and hoping for an answer,
from that one who sits on high, remove us from this cancer wait up
above there sits his love we all hope we can reach, and every now
and then we see his Dove descending down to teach, those lessons
we did Miss and pass, for reasons choose to kiss away a pain never

meant to last, only with time does bitterness fade that we come to realize, to better honor and seek out that wisdom in the eyes of those who have walked those harsher roads that always lay ahead that task to change we found was strange, ambition had once Led.........

# Cast from a dream

## Perry Sisk-December 2023

*There are great pillars around this world we have known, some cast in marble are hewn granite and stone, many set amidst the sea above an below that few ever see, these monuments of time manifesting divine by how they were built some set in one line, made to depict Martyrs of those times lone ago to remind us today our own lifespans may show, countless Evolutions now proven to have been what powers lay beneath one altered skin, confronted then by aggression seemed destined, they too in their time are we sure did they question, their own Fates forseen by profits that has visioned so careful to amass that skill of a surgeon's incision, these we hold high and place above reproach up nowadays they follow suit to gain a seat with a coach, that undermining purpose not seen and not so known until that one hour their cover is blown, so these people we call our leaders today are truly no better than deceit in which they play, to right a wrong that lasted so long indeed require a history said gone, so I guess the point to all that is here said before I put any further thought on this to bed, any measure of time that can be counted by men, brought into the light of the day or by fate is so to end, down through past Generations so few if by number, did hold gifted insights here for the past amidst their slumber, where it not for recall of events they had seen those pillars of past brought forth of a dream..........*

# Spoken clear

## Perry SISK-December 2023

*Here am I by myself thinking there are things we hadn't auto touch
am I so alone in wondering why we didn't learn from past mistakes
that really didn't hurt that much, for being placed into my own
isolation having hopes for a better revelation, sitting here at times
beside myself for the purpose of further speculation, am I alone here
forsake of mounted fear hoping to awakened from a dream that seems
to take me near, to that Edge of time where people stand in line to
be counted off one by one as they disappear into the sun, all these
Visions given me across an Open Sea is the telling me it's all a dream
to awaken from be, in the end are we so inclined to give a pass on
what just could not last for anything refined, to include our day-to-
day getting by our plan ahead in hopes to try and just wait out for a
lasting heavy sigh, was I the only one to wait for truth be told of the
many hearts and Minds and willingness be sold, some are singled out
I guess separated from the rest to leave a mark Somewhere in Time
a heavy heart inside my chest, will yet be something of value to pass
along but along to who will be better determined by those who wrote
the song, still waiting to be written much less ever being heard and so
was captured in his word clearly spoken not once but a third.........*

# One shirt I wore

## Perry Sisk-December 2023

*I made it out to my door today to head out to the store, and hopes to buy a shirt to wear, the other day I tore, not to buy those common goods but just one item needed, nor go on any shopping spree the owner of the store had needed, there was a time I knew to sew and repair such things myself, but now as Eyesight Fades and though those threads and needles I put upon a shelf, now some may ask what makes this an issue to want to go on about, the subtle reminder of my age my Prime I once did Tout, now bare in mind some give no credence for this simple shirt I bought one simple garment we all do where, but this held one special thought, this shirt I had hoped to find the same pattern it did hold not all shirts are meant for show or keep us from the cold, for this one shirt was giving me one who held a place, when I wear it day or night it reminds me of a face, this face of one departed now was one time my best friend for this reason I hold onto that kindness this shirt does send, have you not heard it said there are days we dread to one day Walk Alone, this shirt I have spoken of came from one as close as one within my home, a loss of pain that time won't mend until again I see one measured kindness lent the shirt I wear replaced with care it says to honor one, that now resides along with both our father and his son.........*

# A heart to enter

## Perry Sisk - December 2023

What gives some that fortitude
To endure and reach their best
Is it as clever not to elude
That total patient test
Some hold a will from where to instill
That trait so ingrained
Just as sorrow for grave loss
Can leave one's face tear stained
Emotion play that awkward way
That few can hold at bay
At times we see and often hear
What no words found can say
Not too often do we find
That which will leave us guessing
To be forced to unlearn those things
That we learned would truly be one blessing
I guess and suppose it takes a gift
That is handed from above
To stay headstrong be right be wrong
If all for the sake of love

*Love when tempted to walk both sides*
*Of a fence or have that cake and eat it too*
*We come to realize just who we knew*
*And yet still wonder who*
*Lord keep inside we found where to hide*
*That heart we broke into..........*

# Something sought after

## Perry Sisk - December 2023

*You know it is pretty much a safe bet that I've reached this conclusion before, there are many was and as there are so many ways to ignore, do I pick a window to jump out of or do I just choose another door, either way it be there could be more to see were it not for open-mindedness or allow door idle thought so many to cross a path is it fruitless anyway, some would have me be so inclined to seek out inspirations far better or so defined, to be impartial with one's thoughts should leave far less be desired when given that our time at best as stated how we are wired, even found one common ground within our mind is true, we think to share with standing there that one that always knew, I once was likened to a puzzle with pieces never placed, to fined that comfort for myself, was one thing always chased..........*

# So simple a plan

## Perry Sisk-December 2023

Did our father hold a brush to paint our world and too, did that father hold a bucket to pour the oceans blue, when our father in Heaven hung the skies above did he also fill our heart with never-ending love, did that Master of creation give color to all those singing birds did he set our lands amidst the water be measured by one thirds, did God create the winds whereby clouds to do always chase a sky so blue they fall away at night they hide in haste, did our Lord put into place all these wonders be to cause our minds to ponder if there will be much more to see, these things God placed onto our world both high above and low, all the many simple things that in his wisdom for all to bestow.

# A garden so tended

## Perry Sisk-December 2023

When the bloom falls away and an infant fruit appears, one child as a melon on the vine amidst an array of fears, a lack of rain give dread of drought, and two without sunshine one fails to grow so Stout, onward to fall with caution of Frost, we hope to be gathered before we are lost, to apply this way of thinking to all that are born, that Vines so attached detached from the scorn, the value of men is not measured by deed but rather good soil so prompted by seed, the influence of seasons disrupted and wrong, for who knows the reason once written in song, this Garden of Life God put into place that all he has tended show frown to his face, all things he made living will be known by it's fruit, that vine from which we began will never dispute, adhering to Faith to worship His name That harvested Garden God planted the same.........

# Merely a notion

## Perry Sisk–November 2023

Those that are gifted in voice are sometimes asked to sing us home, that artist talented with a brush is sought to paint a picture of a temple set near Rome, folks who are taught a surgical skill are often said to mend the will some that are practiced in knowledge or deemed to be a learned class, are a few directed to Simply teach and be transparent as glass, for nothing abstains as a purpose foretold being mild of temperament as well as so bold, few things in one's life was never achieved that lack grit and strive so many believe, trust in one's self sometimes handed down by advice or by Guidance few others thought sound, still waters run deep but also reflect those secrets just to walk in the sun amidst our own a smile we refrain while some we outright shun, there are times that I asked if I'm alone on this stage where family and friends together actors left holding no wage these hours that I spend at times so disheartened I miss, those days of true innocence as that child mom would kiss, away all the pain and the fear of unknown not hearing that patients of voice till when I was grown, if one tonic could fix or repair all I see no Elixir or potion will ever set free, as everyone else is meant to be me merely a notion..........

# Stay our damnation

## Perry Sisk - November 2023

*Will common sense save this generation that lost they repeat and they rinse their skills at high cost, given to choose left or turn right, one leads into the eye still will yield truth though most will deny, those who allow evil to hold in it's place may be just as complicit to join in it's race, thereby failing to gain any Grace, those who Bend the truth to meet their own needs should always be seen as that snake in the weeds, do we not hear those Whispers that voice to always be given that will of One's Choice, the elders that held that moral fiber now rare this young of the present stand distant and dare, those that were linger in hopes of better change before that one moral compass becomes ever so strange, remember so fondly that love had no condition, be their will to survive, or to see true perdition..........*

# One roaming spirit

## Perry Sisk - April 2023

*How often have we heard time sure does fly on by nowadays as many would say just as much for asking why, as a child the hours dragged on so slow we feared there was no end later on those hearts we broke were feared to never mend, those hearts repaired with love so shared forever and a time, a clock that strikes we fail to wind well always lose it's chime, now at Mid age we searched the stage that act we once portrayed that impatience we held so long ago shelved now leave us betrayed, those days that took forever to pass when in our youth did we always take for granted companionship we have missed not long for resides a living proof these days I spend alone inside an empty home will soon one day serve to justify a spirits need to roam..........*

# Where a soul hides

## Perry Sisk–February 2024

Think for a moment what is there to see when we step from behind that one tall single tree, a tree and a forest of soulless delusion from which there has been planted that darkest illusion, one that's been shared by another is shown harbored deceptions so long it has been, by chance unobserved gave relevance for in darkness they are captured so near to the door, those forested should long shielded in shade of trees tall and numbered with obscurity they made, some may ask where are you going with this here by only pointing out what's been obvious we miss, those times that we walk through woods to find peace that stillness we assume no greater place to reside and keeps us immune, here these souls that endured the torment and pain will one day so join—that forest of God's reign..........

# Will of the heart

## Perry d Sisk - no date given

Just how often have we always heard it said
Well the writing's on the wall
No more secrets to be shed
Drawn to one conclusion as an ending to a play
Comes now that final curtain call
With more words to say
Do we not all view our lives as such
Those times forgotten for who we touched
By words or thoughts begotten so much
A rose to share or ever dare to clutch
For if there were a rose so known by any other name
It was found for lack of fortune
Or even hope of fame
So sticking to and older adage all things in time will be
For none will know the ebb and flow of tides upon the sea
Sometimes we see an open heart be seen as much the same
Long before it passes through
That bitterness and shame
For all too often took for granted that compassion it could share
Knowing not for whom it broke would still hold one care

*Resilient and ways one cannot define or cast a light on still*
*So fragile too was known by few for holding to it's will*
*This will he gives to all who lives maintain his love apart*
*From them that keep their open heart.........*

# One penny of gold

## Perry Sisk –

I remember as a child my grand ma used to say a penny for your
thoughts she would ask on any given day, not knowing then the
what or when I would come to understand, her wisdom deep
as any ocean now sees this older man, how was it known where
winds had blown to praise her still today, a gift inside she said
I would hide until I too was old and gray, while memories fade
those of Grandma that stayed I have held this fondness for, my
grandma's true kindness went past all the blindness as she passed
through Heaven's Door, this I know to be true for there are others
that see it too, those thoughts to many in every counted penny if
she would see I seen she knew, one penny turned to gold...........

# That window to look through

## Perry Sisk-January 2024

Just a few things to address and unpack if you will, picture
elbows placed upon a single window sill, gazing through the
pain and that bigger picture there, of all there is to see and
hold within one captured stare, what is more to want then all
we have at present being, these wonders of our lives he gives
and all that we are seeing, some are content to abide with
what they have with never a need to pursue and to strive, for
all they call that fortune of fame yet even and that we remain
the same and alive, I believe all truly hold the essence of what
is good, not only for self but for any that would, take note of
promotion so why does an ocean to further endow ones love and
devotion, to all that's been given so freely o cost to feel a need
for anything more what show just what was lost, one sense of
humility it took years to attain and looking out upon all that
has been, a given received through this window pain..........

# Where did the father stand

Perry Sisk--November 2023

Are there times in looking back toward we choose to use giving description of one many thoughts we always wish to lose so many depictions given cause for revelation leaving outlets to disengage or ever abandoned one's true station, though try in vain to regain composure from failure we endure yet disregard for efforts sake so often claimed was pure, these mortal eyes that search the skies and gaze out toward a star or Father's hand alone that placed them there, his door was left a jar, his spirit given all to one task to bare alone, one bleak though bitter history shown, also said men's Hearts will faint this change of landscape our Lord will paint, those that prosper over ill-gotten gain shall to the wayside there and never touched by rain, for all there has been or will be to see one always present constant

My father stood with me

# Stillness of time

Perry Sisk—October 2023

This I have come to know as passions do degrade, conviction though stay constant as mountains on a horizon Forever cast their shade, not to let this confused with Broad and deep compassion a love for all things living for surpass what man will ever fashion, instinct so Bound By Nature inside of every being, just one day past and those forthcoming do always hold the Sun, just as the Moon will shift the tides of every sea and ocean, I look upon a tapestry of night those pinprick stars with light, we see those patterns called by name that cast and darkness sky where one canvas painted with delight by whose hand held the brush of creation tells all of God his might, here in comes the answer accept it if you will, who holds those reigns of all we know and marks our time stand still..........

# Did he know

Perry Sisk-no date

It's hard at times to address of find or pin down just where it started, the cause for which unto a switch to leave one Brokenhearted, all the while did fake the smile to show I'm getting by, though in a mirror there stays the fear that lack of tears deny, I guess out of anger I find a stranger within myself was felt, a future programed and still recessed that I was dealt, no one ever knew or ever did see through that shadow kept well hidden, to curse that day I lost my way the road I took forbidden, so blinded to those few that ever knew what passage of time will play, throughout this life and into the next is when I'll hear him say, this was not your choice or mine to voice for you up-and-coming of a age, just understand that in his plan it's one who turns the page, something hidden and shielded away that hurt that I kept buried even then and still today, this thing that came about in my later teenage years as I grew near to know him better and what caused all his fears, my dad for most accounts was nearing middle age and I guess at forty seven with no thought to leave this stage, I hear it said time and again far too young to go, even now well past his age I still cannot say I know, why he was taken all too soon in many people's eyes, I have asked myself and strict delusion as I have looked up to the skies, for just one answer for what the reason was this allowed to be I guess too young and not the season why be shown to me, so with that I have waited as so was stated with wisdom one passes past an age, filled with knowledge not to question though accept what youth cannot gauge, folks spoke of things that sometimes happen but never do they know why some will live in a shadow of heir fathers even after their called to go, still yet from then and to this day I have no answer for so in this way one has to say what future holds in store, for those that are taken up before their time that we still so often measure, never really know until that faded glow of those we lose we treasure, both day and night my mind did fight to gain an understanding to that mystery of those early years and here and at times no shed of tears I still think dad you knew.........

# Truth be told

## Perry Sisk - September 2023

*Dear father of our heavens may we see you high upon those clouds of white high Aloft that Eastern sky, that day that Satan's hold will end and even he will bow a sight foretold of prophets declaring thus endow, for those that held to one belief who have stood on all this while, that day which ends all sadness and grief be shown by all who smile, some call it a vision some say that they did dream that Nations one by one will fall upon his glory final scene, when seeds of doubt say there is no life after death where then did the soul of man happen upon his breath, as God created this tapestry of life this Earth has canvas did paint upon where in his word so stated his light applied unto all the land, with waters deep is cast by every Dawn, his son has shown on every man one light that can't be hidden, for in the hearts and minds of all good that follow an end to be forbidden*

*Truth be told.*

# His love endures

Perry Sisk - June 2024

If given an audience with the man upstairs
I would ask why sometimes it seems he often seldom cares
Given he knew us while still in the womb
Why are we giving a life that ends all too soon
And too I would ask caretaker of all there has been
There is and will be
Why are we made so fragile in body and mind
With things we cannot see
So many are the questions I'd have for God above
Like why from a time of conception
We're anointed with his love
As we come into the world and said to be unique
For all within their own rights
We were taught it is his kingdom we should seek
I'd also need to ask
While it is true we are resilient too
We still are held to account
For things we never knew
Those laws God handed down
For all to know and keep

*No one living then Nor today*
*For breaking them what is to reap*
*Being mortal and so easily deceived*
*How does one Escape their condemnation*
*Less foregoing our own guilt*
*How do we bypass incrimination*
*Still in all with all of this*
*here this one thing will I always miss*
*That loving embrace one gives to another*
*If for no other reason that to say*
*God's loves endures forever..........*
*Amen*

# A choice

Perry Sisk - May 2024

This freedom to be free was not placed on Humanity by men alone that caused unrest

That still the heart within his chest, Free will alone was given men to choose to ponder not to sin

For in this concept do we find, a future Mocks the past that has been, the lessons learned from failure

Are doomed to be repeated just as history reflects those lessons seldom heeded, when becoming obsolete

Indignation in full retreat, if those values held in high esteem seeming less to be concrete.

With words that hold far different meaning a pasture of wheat in need of Gleening, before the winds

May put to waste that very life we have yet to ever taste, a condescending nature creates obscurity in reason

*What would man subsist upon were it not for every season, philosophers of old always tortured always cold*

*Premise for a Sacred Heart seldom realized before we're old, lastly stated here is said each new day we make our bed*

*Dreams we recall and recite with a voice lends to offer one final choice*

*A choice of losing freedom to be free..........*

# What will be shown

## Perry d Sisk - June 2024

As we spouse being filled with good intentions
Less we forgot any weighted measure of preventions
As told by history in and of itself
All things even Justice
Gathers dust when placed upon a shelf
Still there are those that wear upon what is Holy
If allowed time to improve and correct
Mistakes they made solely
Out of righteous errors made in jest
Never understanding they had failed to pass one test
What then will be offered up as recompense
For our time in Memorial
What has been the same ever since
All the many things of this life our minds says leave alone
Will soon enough haunt our hearts to find or recall
Those things to atone
That one day will be shown

# One Worldly View

A personal view of ones life is neither here nor there

In larger scheme of things far too many just won't care

Looking back on errors made while sitting beneath this tree amidst its shade

Far be it known for there is much to atone before those memories fade

For those that view life and this world a learning stage

Those who depart early from it with no time to earn a wage

Need no fear encompass those remained upon this stage

Lessons learned throughout one's life meant to be passed on

To others yet to fill the shoes so many now are gone

what they take to another possible Realm

Truly makes one Wonder who pilots this ship it's helm

To Endeavor risk the loss of one's conviction

Should truly be so set apart that lack of ones restriction

Often words will explain away what mystery we endure

Nonetheless within it we find one cure

Take not for granted those things you cannot see

One's viewpoint ever so slanted gave cause for what's to be

# One marker to be

## Perry d Sisk-July 2024

What must I do that most of this life is through what choice is there but to wait on the day nothing much more to offer in any given way as I walked down the road I see edged in purple a simple subtle Breeze sweeps across those blossoms of crepe myrtle so simple a thing to notice some I am sure would insist and yet so taken for granted these things we dare not list yet these days I spend now and at times in disbelief just where or when or how my departure will find relief relieved in knowing there was nothing more to take from one that outlived usefulness they would say For Heaven's Sake and too I'd like to think before that final setting of the Sun that all in all this life did teach I will hear a job well done for if we are put here to learn from life all things no one can measure this alone I'd write in stone what more would Treasure they're also was a time I heard it said you are wise beyond your years yet little did anyone know back when I challenge most all my fears I suppose and answer comes with time to most concerns concealed just to know and apple tastes so sweet he stays red before it is filled so herein lies all the wherefore and why's I still will leave alone one name and two dates was something else said upon this one headstone..........

# One Light

## Perry d Sisk - Jul 2024

As the light of day presents itself upon the waters and streams

Just as memories fade that pertained to ending dreams

As with just one hour before the stars
that shined above and beyond

They too reflected their passions upon lakes and pond

Far and wide be it noted inside, everyone is skin or related in pride

Always is the case to obscure and erase those
feelings thoughts we'd otherwise wish to hide

Given true and bitter observance of this what more
would stand out as something in all is still amiss

We're it not for prophets of old their stories
forecast their fables foretold

History shows it is doomed to be repeated as the
seeing what is just so often be deleted a stone we find
in darkness is always stumbled upon fearing a fall
we all may take for sake of what was wrong

Yes there are times one has little to right and too there are
times ones choice is to fight there are days to pick up a pen and
write though words on paper will rarely bring any to light

At times it is seen through fog covered lense a heart
that is done wrong so much harder to cleanse

At any given time this is found to be so ones
spirit soars high then brought to its low

Those that are deemed as truly inventive

So rare to be found endorsed by incentive

Those that will stand for what is good and just so often
passed by and their views so commonly never discussed

They too did leave a legacy obscured by so many that
failed to understand or heed what most had endured
a truth that light brings in his will be assured

# A love all ways

## Perry d Sisk Sep 2024

When in time in observance of our past things we chose
to do things we thought would last when will we in
number be tested upon which day some saw that one
had rested taking heed to what things went not seen
or even heard knowing full well a song and fight does
belong to a bird seek we now that wisdom to discern and
never question what more is to learn for in remembrance
of all things we let go those people and places so dear
and we know so many may ask why am I here then
go on to ponder is it anguish or joy that is found in a
tear now in wonderment of who here is writing this
test of time has bestowed upon a degree of relevance
found with such inciting given who I am or another
I may have been that has had a life so encompassed
with mistakes and more so even sin for alone I am not
nor by countless others they too must have been the
keepers of their brothers thus in this Final Chapter of
living and endurance of so often and at times did feel
the Sorrows of failed love in so much now captures
and holds that Tightest Bond those I never knew yet

still did Miss like ripples of a stone cast into a pond all those little simple gestures so often took for granted just knowing these things come back around to show our view was slanted all these thoughts conveyed herein I know apply to others just as love was never constrained by our fathers and our mothers all ways..........

# Ones Cup of Reflection

## perry d risk Sep 024

I come into this world in the decade of the 50s those that brought me up said be Leary of the 60s high school and the 70s came my way those late teen years like my dad they passed away no one knows those reasons for why to question what was brings heavy a sigh getting past that grief and loss I cannot say when or even if I ever did I Ponder now and then on throughout the 80s are done what most will do most would say like Johnny come lately only few that knew while time progressed and my convictions compressed those 90s were much the same though with all my arrogance and prideful resolve myself I stand to blame the year 2000 lay just ahead what more there was to dread thinking of ways of getting by I dwelled on this instead take note my friend for in the end there is far worse one can imagine looking back on things I'd change it's easier to fight a dragon so this I conclude as I try to elude what is best left so unsaid these dreams are awaken from time to time seemed never to leave my bed with all of what's been and still I miss every now and then those years growing up and picture this there is still one empty cup summing up I miss..........

www.ingramcontent.com/pod-product-compliance
Lightning Source LLC
Chambersburg PA
CBHW020919140626
46545CB00015B/939